Grandma's Guide to Child Care

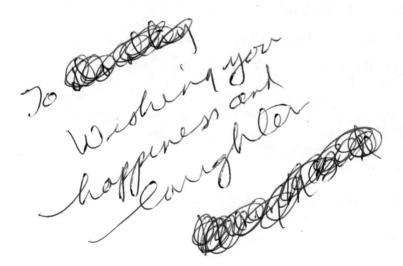

To *[signature]*
Wishing you
happiness and
laughter
[signature]

Library of Congress Cataloguing-in-Publication Data

Satire

Copyright @ 1990 by Mary McBride

Library of Congress No. 90-082787

ISBN No.: 0-9627601-0-2

Authors: Mary McBride and Veronica McBride

Illustrator: Christine Tripp

Editor: Helen Duffy

Published by The Brothers Grinn, Chicago, IL

About the Authors: Mary McBride has been a gag writer for Phyllis Diller and Joan Rivers and is one of the busiest and funniest speakers in America. She and her daughter, Veronica McBride, have also written *Grandma Knows Best, But No One Ever Listens!*, *Don't Call Mommy at Work Today Unless the Sitter Runs Away*, and *The Empty Nest Symphony.*

About the Illustrator: Christine Tripp has illustrated the previous McBride books and lives with her husband and four children in Ottawa, Canada.

Table of Contents

Table of Contents 2

Chapter 1

A Pregnancy Diagnosis Doesn't Need a Second Opinion

Pregnancy brings morning sickness
It will also swell you.
And though your husband loves you
He will never spell you.

Unless she is an adoptive mother every grandmother has gone through pregnancy and it is regretful her experience is not used more to benefit present mothers-to-be.

The following is some grandmotherly information:

Pregnancy can be an enjoyable experience. Don't think of it only in the negative — as being taken off the Threat to Other Women list for five months or being forced to by-pass wet T-shirt contests.

Mothers-to-be immediately start fixing up a bedroom for the baby. It would be better if they began by fixing up the bathroom as that is the room where they will be spending a great deal of time.

Adjustment is the key word. Be calm about the changes that occur in your body — not like the pregnant woman who said, "What was that?!" **every** time the baby kicked.

As soon as it is not just a hunch you must tell your husband you're pregnant. You can't get by with writing it in your diary and hoping that he will snoop.

1

Try to be a little creative in making the announcement. The following are a few suggestions of fresh ways to say, "I'm going to have a baby!"

- "How about cutting back on the garden next year and putting up a swing set?"

- "You know how you always complain that all the good movies are on in the middle of the night? Now you will be able to watch them."

- "Don't you think it's about time we started to get some use out of the leaves for the table?"

- "Would you consider trading your 10-speed bike for a 3-speed with a baby seat?"

- "Want to have an excuse to leave a boring party?"

Be creative in announcing your pregnancy.

- "How would you like to give your niece a little cousin?"

- "Want to get more out of Father's Day?"

- In the supermarket put five jars of pickles in the cart.

- If he is changing channels during a baby product commercial say, "Don't turn."

- Give him an empty frame and say, "In nine months you can put this on your desk with a picture of a baby in it."

- On the bathroom wall write, "MARGARET SANGER IS A RAT FINK."

Send a telegram to your mother and mother-in-law to inform them. Telegrams can arrive simultaneously while with a telephone call one will have to be informed before the other.

You will no doubt talk to your obstetrician to learn about the development of a fetus but there may be some information a grandmother can pass on that a doctor will not impart.

- Early detection means nothing.

- A silver knife does not keep down the swelling.

- Having plastic surgery on your nose will not prevent the baby from having a nose like yours.

- The mind of a pregnant woman is full of red diagonal lines — cigarettes ... coffee ... liquor.

If you want to take time to smell the roses ask someone to pick them so you don't have to bend over.

The following are some more hints that take your condition into consideration:

- Use only beach towels after a bath.

- Buy a How to Remove Stains book as you will be constantly spilling food on your stomach.

3

- Have an unlisted phone number to cut down on the number of times you will have to get up and down.

- If you plan to get a bigger house after the baby comes get it now as you will appear smaller if the house is larger.

- Should you work don't be a clock-watcher. It will make co-workers nervous.

- Always be sure your driveway is clear for delivery trucks who bring things to satisfy your cravings.

- Double knot your shoes when you tie them in the morning.

- Shop in Men's Departments to get outsized garments. (However, don't say to a clerk in a Men's Department, "I'm shopping for maternity clothes.")

There are also some prohibitions involved with this state. The following are a few:

- Just because you are eating for two don't order two portions. If you do at least make one of the orders a child's portion.

- Even though you can't bend over to get a drink from the water fountain don't ask a fellow worker to put his finger over it and spray it up to you.

- It's all right to have your suitcase packed but don't go so far as to equip your car with a siren.

- You can't take your shoes off and soak your feet in a fountain at the mall.

- You can't bring a picture of a baby to your obstetrician and tell him that is what you want your baby to look like.

Pregnant women are all in the same boat (or boats referring to shoes because of swelling). Some typical statements of pregnant women are:

- "I **am** wearing my wedding ring — you just can't see it."

- "When they figure the expenses of raising a child do they count the extra money you spend for getting full service at a gas station."

- "I cried when I looked at the skinny ballerina on my music box."

- "I made the two head holes into one and now I wear the poncho myself that my husband and I used to share at football games."

- "I also have heartburn for two."

- "I made a pink and blue suggestion box so my mother and mother-in-law can write instead of tell me their advice."

- "My husband tried to tell me I was having false cravings."

- "I hate pity. At the open house at my son's school his teacher had me sit at her desk instead of at my child's desk."

There are things you can do to boost your morale during pregnancy:

- Go to the zoo and look at the elephants who have a gestation period of 45 months.

- Shop at the end of the day when the clerks' ankles are also swollen.

- If you are pregnant during Thanksgiving time be sure and watch the Macy's Day Parade to make yourself feel a little less bloated.

On the other hand there are things you should avoid as your morale will be lowered:

- Avoid Toy Departments. You will see children having tantrums.

- Hope your child's teacher doesn't have her pupils draw their mothers at this time.

The time before the baby comes will drag. After the baby is born he or she changes every day so it is interesting. The baby also changes every day before it is born but these changes cannot be observed unless you have daily ultra-sound pictures taken.

Chapter 2

Who Gave Me the Mother Goose Night Light?

Absent is the donor
Of the gift you clutch.
You still do "ooh" and "ahh"
But maybe not as much.

Tradition has it you will be given a baby shower.

People who give baby showers ought to be handed a list of suggestions of things to do that would make the mother-to-be enjoy the shower more:

- Ask everyone to wear loose-fitting clothing so there aren't any 20-inch waists in view.

- Make sure that the only chair left for the guest of honor to sit on isn't a fragile antique.

- Award a prize to the person who comes up with the longest list of baby-sitters.

- Make assembling the gifts which need assembling a shower game.

At a baby shower, be sure that no more than two people help the guest of honor out of a chair.

- When bringing in chairs from the other room bring in an extra chair for the mother-to-be's swollen feet.

- Be sure that not more than two people help the guest of honor out of a chair.

- Don't have an outdoor shower. An insect bite could make the mother-to-be swell even more.

This isn't maximum comfort time for you so there may be some unpleasantness connected with a baby shower. Once a guest sat on the gift of a squeak toy and sent the guest of honor into labor.

- A gift of a potty chair could make you have to go to the bathroom.

7

- You may fall sound asleep while the music box you received is playing its lullabye.

- The motion of a baby swing may make you sick.

However, the following are a few tips that will enable you to handle your baby shower in the best possible way.

There are certain things you should do to prepare for the shower:

- Clean out your car. Because of your condition guests will help you carry out the gifts and they will see it. Don't take the spare tire out of the trunk as this will make you look too presumptuous.

- Go into the Baby Department of a store and find out what everything is so you don't embarrass yourself by not being able to identify something you receive. Ask the clerk its purpose.

- Do one day's breathing exercise by helping the hostess blow up the pink and blue balloons.

- If you know your doctor's wife request that she be invited to the shower. In case labor starts she will know where to get hold of her husband.

The following are some things to do at the shower so you will get the most out of it:

- Sit next to someone who isn't a mother so you won't hear a scary labor story.

- Prepare them for your thank-you notes being delayed. Say something like, "I've heard that sometimes the swelling doesn't go out of the fingers until weeks after the birth," or "Maybe I'll wait until the baby is old enough to write her own 'Thank You'."

- You will desperately want them to see you after your svelte figure returns. Say, "I want to have a coffee so you can see the baby."

- Don't find out the price of the group gift and divide it by the number of guests, tempting as it is.

- Take a picture of the shower cake to show your doctor so he'll be kind about your weight gain.

The most important thing of all is being enthusiastic about the presents you receive.

The following are a few samples of gracious remarks about gifts:

- "This baby will be so outstanding I know I'm going to need all four of these baby books."

- "Oh, good! Another baby scale. You can't have enough baby scales."

If you have another child arrange to have him out of the house when you come in with all those presents for somebody else.

Chapter 3

Handle the Handle with Care

Even though the Birth Announcement
Must be sent on time
To write, "Name will follow later"
Wouldn't be a terrible crime.

If only babies came named! How nice it would be if the doctor would hand you your child and say, "Here is your new little daughter Lisa" or "Here is your son David."

But of course this is not the case so the parent must bear the responsibility of selecting a name that will not be a handicap to the child.

Parents are understandably very worried about making a mistake in this important task of naming. One mother was so insecure about her choice she thought that might be the reason the baby cried so much. She'd ask, "Hungry?", "Wet diaper?" or "Hates his name?".

Much thought must be put into this part of parenting. You should think of their holding up lines in banks and grocery stores while they are made to spell a name that is very unusual. Consider that maybe she wouldn't raise her hand in school because she doesn't want the teacher to call out that name.

Not only do you have to think about the child himself liking the name — you have to think about how your other children will like it as you'll probably often accidentally call them that name.

There are many things that can be done to aid you in making a good choice of a name:

- It helps to see it written. Write it on a lunch bag. Put it on a birthday cake. Make a fake birth certificate with that name filled in.
- Ask someone in a department store to call that name out over the loud-speaker to see how it sounds if the child gets lost.
- Have an artist sketch what your baby will look like as an adult and name that.
- Suggest that a game at your baby shower be giving favorite names.
- Ask the mailman some of the nice names he has seen on envelopes.
- Give your daughter a name that has various spellings so she can choose a spelling she likes.
- Think how a young sibling could mispronounce that name as that could be what the child is called.

Giving a child an old-fashioned name won't mean she will have old-fashioned morals.

- Go to a playground and call out the name you are considering. If more than 10 children come running it is too popular.

- Write "Dr.", Atty.", or "Rev." in front of it. For instance, Dr. Bambi Smith, Atty. Taffy Anderson or Rev. Brandy Wilson would not be good. Remember that they may not want to go into show business.

Have unlimited dreams for your child and give a name that would go well with a Park Avenue address. The Second sounds better than Jr. If you find it difficult to call your child John Smith II think of the child being a sequel and sequels are always known as II, III, or IV.

If after nine months of arguing the only name you and your husband agree on doesn't go well with your last name, change your name.

There are dangerous practices regarding the name of a child. The following are a few things to avoid:

- Don't wait until you get to the hospital to choose the name. You are liable to name it after any person who makes you more comfortable. It could be Oscar the Custodian who helped you get a can of pop out of the vending machine.

- Don't let another child in the family pick the name. They might have a secret case of sibling rivalry.

- Don't give your child the name of a soap opera star. You'll be accused of being a couch potato.

- Don't pick a name that has a rhyming word that could become a taunt — like Crazy Daisy.

- Don't give a girl a double name if your last name is a hyphenated name. She could marry a man with a hyphenated name and it wouldn't all fit in blanks.

Biblical names, names that got changed at Ellis Island, quotations about names such as "A Rose by any other name.." and "He who steals my purse steals trash, but who steals my good name...." point out the importance of a name.

The following is some more name information:

- You can't make up a name and have it copyrighted.
- A child doesn't care in the least what the name means.
- Grandparents like names that were popular in another era. However, they use terms of endearment instead of the name anyhow.
- Giving a child a name he will like is not spoiling him.
- If you don't use a common spelling of a name people will think the child doesn't know how to spell his own name.
- First name spellings are changed to sound less American like Maria instead of Mary. Last names are changed to sound more American.
- Giving a child an old-fashioned name won't mean she will have old-fashioned morals.
- A parent prefers the question "Where did I come from?" to "Why did you name me that?"
- Di and Charles had the right idea. They gave their boys so many names there is bound to be one they like.
- A good reason not to take the fertility pill is having to face the problem of thinking of so many names.

You can't whisper the name to the child in the womb and if she kicks you'll know she doesn't like it. It is a matter of luck as to whether the name will be a winner with her. To take away some of the pressure in selecting a name it might help to realize there are some advantages to giving children names they hate:

- He'll drive more carefully so he won't have to show his name on his driver's license.
- She won't be so eager to write checks.
- He'll be happy to see mail addressed "OCCUPANT".
- She won't fight over top billing on a marquee.
- He'll get out of bed quicker so you won't keep calling that name.

Chapter 4

Don't Stay with Me — Go Out and Line Up Baby-sitters!

The father would be led into the waiting room
There he would proceed to pace
<u>Now</u> he's brought into the delivery room
Where he's apt to faint and fall upon his face.

When you start having to soap your shoes off and you pop laces on running shoes it's time to have the baby.

You can wait for the perfect moment to tell your husband you're going to have a baby but you can't wait for the perfect moment to tell him it's on the way.

When a baby decides to be born his determination is awesome. You must get in the car immediately and head for the hospital. A couple of no-no's are:

- If your other children are fighting don't postpone your departure until the argument is settled.

- Don't finish stenciling the Mickey Mouse characters on the nursery wall.

- Don't get a sub for your bridge club.

Sometimes husbands seem insensitive.

- Don't stop at a TYME machine to get money for your husband's cigarettes.
- Don't listen to the end of a song before you get out of the car.

If the computer is down when you get to the hospital you can't say to the admitting clerk, "I'll go home and you can call me when it's back up."

Even though you've been around for over 20 years you are going into an unfamiliar and exciting new phase of your life. You could make some embarrassing mistakes.

The following are a few warnings so you don't make a fool of yourself:

- If another one of your doctor's patients is in the labor room at the same time you don't flip a coin to see who gets him.
- Don't send a birth announcement to the doctor who delivered the baby. He already knows.
- Don't send an announcement to the proprietor of the GETAWAY MOTEL where the baby was conceived.

- Don't put a description of the birth on the birth announcement.
- Don't call your boss from the delivery room to let him know the exact moment your maternity leave starts.
- Don't call the mayor to tell him to change the population sign.
- You can't pre-register at the hospital.
- Just because you don't think you'll have an accurate record of the baby's development if the baby doesn't get weighed on the same scale, you shouldn't ask to buy the delivery room scale.
- Don't bring your baby book into the delivery room so you can record whose finger he grabbed first.
- Don't call everyone in your address book when you go into labor.

When all the principal players are in place it's embarrassing to have the pains stop but this often happens. It is called false labor.

Hospitals would do well to advertise, "We cater to false labor". It could be miserable if someone said, "Are you the little Mommy-to-be who cries 'Wolf'?" or if you were asked for a list of references who could vouch that you aren't the type to go to the hospital when it isn't the real thing.

When you leave for the hospital say in a loud voice that your neighbors will hear, "Have you got the grocery list?" so you won't be embarrassed if it turns out to be false labor.

You can't ask the hospital if you can leave some of the things from your suitcase there until you come back.

Some husbands are not as handy as others. For instance one about-to-be father poked his finger in his wife's eye as he was mopping her brow.

There are also those men who are not as handy with words. Of course it is very difficult to know what is exactly the right thing to say at this time. Hopefully he would know enough not to say, "Ouch!" when she squeezes his hand.

The following are some examples of dangerous delivery discourse:
- "Have the nurse motion me to come in if it's the real thing."

- "I'm taking notes so you can study them and do better next time."
- "These people want to get out of here. Can't you hurry?"
- "I'm ready to snap your picture — smile!"
- "Don't you want to be a role model for the young nurses around here?"
- "Are you groaning at my pun?"
- "You're not following the game plan."
- "It's mind over matter."
- "When you got pregnant you made a commitment to go through with this."
- "It's like a picnic — you keep saying, 'It's not coming out' like you do with ketchup."
- "Well you don't want to spend the rest of your life pregnant, do you?"

A husband should say, "I just wish I could take some of the pain". Of course he may get a punch or a bite.

As with any situation the more information you have the better. The following are some more facts about delivering a baby:

- Loving to be the center of attention doesn't help.
- It is the ideal time to discuss a major purchase you've been wanting to make.
- If the doctor examines you with binoculars the head is not down far enough.
- You cannot depend on your husband being with you during the delivery.
- He could make a dash for the door or faint.
- Don't bring a Size 3 dress to wear home from the hospital. You'll be more comfortable in maternity clothing. Should it be a top that says "BABY" with an arrow pointing to your stomach write "NO" in front of "BABY".
- After you've had the baby there will be so many people to thank — the doctor, the nurses, all the people who have been helping you out of chairs, and people who picked up things you dropped to name a few.
- With a snip of the umbilical cord you are permitted to have post partem depression.

Though there is some unpleasantness about giving birth there are also things for which to be thankful:

- Your obstetrician doesn't charge by the hour which would make a long labor more painful.

- Your obstetrician wears a mask so you can't tell if he's looking concerned.

- You can't be banned from the hospital after so many false labors.

- If you have to drive yourself to the hospital even if it is a long distance there is no danger of you falling asleep.

When it is time to go to the hospital don't think only of yourself. Your husband will also be going through a lot. You will know your husband is upset if he offers a $500 reward to anyone who finds your suitcase.

Chapter 5

The Baby Won't Call the Sitter Mommy after an Hour

The first evening out after Baby
Will be far from being top-notch
If you look less at the face of your husband
Than you look at the face of your watch.

You can't wait until the child is old enough to dial 911 himself to have an evening out. It is only fair to you and your husband to go out by yourselves for some socialibility soon after the baby is born.

The first time you get a sitter and leave your precious baby behind will be very traumatic. Therefore it is important that you make it as easy on yourself as possible. The following are a few suggestions:

- Don't dress the baby in her most becoming outfit. It will be harder to leave her.

- Eat at a restaurant where there will be loud music so you can't hear sirens.

- Go out with another couple so your husband will have someone to talk to while you make phone calls home.

- Write the number where you can be reached on places where the sitter is sure to see it such as a mirror, the potato chip box, or the refrigerator.

19

- When you call home take the baby-sitter's word that everything is all right. Don't insist she put the baby on the phone.
- Leave the baby book out. If your baby does anything cute the sitter can write it in.
- Only go to a show that has reserved seating. You can give the sitter your seat number and the usher can find you immediately.

You wouldn't be comfortable being away from your baby the first time if you got your pediatrician to sit. Should your mother sit you'd say, "What do I really know about her?"

While you must be careful about the person to whom you are entrusting your infant don't go overboard. The following are a few samples of going too far:

- Only hiring a sitter with very short hair so hair over her ears doesn't keep her from hearing the baby.
- Only hiring a sitter who has her life-saving certificate.

Some parents are a little too cautious.

- Insisting that she sit in a straight chair all evening so she doesn't get sleepy.
- Stepping back into the house right after you leave and saying, "What's going on here?!" because she's turned on television.
- Warning her about entertaining boyfriends and she's over 70.
- Hiring a sitter with a zilch personality so she won't have any friends to invite over.
- Having an alarm system that will sound if she leaves the house.
- Asking her to move in with you the week before you are going to go out so the baby gets used to her.

While you should relax and have fun you are right not to be too carefree. Here are some precautions you can take:

- Give the sitter a crash course in judo so she can protect your baby against intruders.
- Hide the remote control. Having to get up to change channels will keep her more awake.
- Suggest she watch spook shows. She is less apt to fall asleep.
- Go out on an off night such as Tuesday so your neighbors will be home and your sitter can call them if need be.
- Tell the sitter not to eat peanut butter or caramel. You may not be able to understand her when you call home if she has a mouthful of peanut butter or caramel.
- Don't leave crunch food for her. Chewing it may cause her not to hear the baby.
- Ask if the restaurant or theatre has a PA system that can be heard in the bathroom. If it doesn't don't drink anything.
- List the things for which you want to be called home:

  If he gets the hiccups.
  If he refuses less than 4 ounces of formula.
  If he cries more than five minutes.

21

Enjoy yourself. Don't ruin your time by missing the baby. The following are some things that you could do that would make you be sorry you left home:

- Dining early and seeing other people with children.
- Looking at the crackers on the table and thinking of a baby eating a soda cracker.
- Reading "CHILDREN'S PORTIONS" on the menu.

Also you should be careful not to ruin your evening by imagining terrible things happening:

- Don't leave more than one box of Band-Aids.
- Don't leave a tourniquet.
- Don't get a car phone installed just so the sitter will be able to reach you while you are getting there and coming home.
- Don't check the date your sitter's CPR course completed.

The evening will seem endless but you must make an effort not to spoil your husband's time by rushing to get back home:

- Don't go to the kitchen door at the restaurant and yell, "Hurry up in there!"
- Don't tell your husband your fortune cookie says, "Get home to your baby as fast as you can".
- Don't pretend you hate the movie so you can leave. You could spend a miserable Oscar night watching it get 10 awards.

However there are things you can do so the evening won't be prolonged so long you get nervous:

- Choose a restaurant that is known more for its fast service than for its good food.
- Order the special as that always gets served quicker.
- Don't dally over choices. Say, rapid fire, "Soup, thousand island, baked" right after telling what entree you want.
- Don't order dessert. Tell your husband there are mints in the car to eat on the way home.
- Wear dark glasses so people won't recognize you and stop to visit.
- Put your coat on the back of your chair instead of checking it.
- Get a lot of change so you'll be able to leave the correct amount to pay your bill and take right off.

It's too bad restaurants and theatres don't offer baby-sitting services.

Chapter 6

No, You Won't Pollute the Water by Going in the Toilet

It's not hard to explain
Why I'm a griper —
He's nearly three
and he goes in his diaper.

A baby-sitter who specialized in toilet training would be deluged with requests for her services.

The hardest part of raising children is getting them out of diapers.

It is a known fact that a child under two wants to be moving every second. Therefore they begrudge the time they have to sit still to fulfill the obligation of elimination. They wait until the last minute to head for the bathroom, often incorrectly estimating what is the last minute.

It is war and the child must surrender but he fights a terrific battle.

With disposable diapers available mothers today are not in such a rush to teach their little ones to go on the potty. However when your mother or mother-in-law gives training pants for gifts it is probably time to get to toilet trainings.

23

***To make her tinkle, try crying. Maybe the water
from your eyes will do the trick.***

So you will know that other mothers experience the same difficulties as you do in accomplishing this feat the following are some examples of mothers' statements during toilet training:

- "When I was nine months' pregnant I wouldn't buck a restroom line. If my two-year old says, 'I gotta go potty', I will."
- "I said to her, 'Aren't your little legs falling asleep sitting there so long? Mine are'."
- "There should be Congratulations on Getting your Child Trained cards."
- "I must say, now that he's older he's more interesting to sit beside for hours."
- "Well at least **my** hips don't seem as big while she's wearing rubber pants over a diaper."
- "I spend more time in the bathroom than a teen-age girl."
- "It's a shame getting your child toilet trained isn't news you can put in the Christmas letter."

24

The following are some suggestions to assist you in this exasperating chore:

- Stop playing peek-a-boo while changing him.
- Start an afghan and work on it while you are sitting beside the potty chair waiting for things to happen.
- If you don't knit or crochet read while sitting there. It is too depressing to do nothing and notice all the flaws in the bathroom.
- Ask for tips from someone you see buying training pants or from someone giving a rummage sale and selling a potty chair.
- To make her tinkle try crying. Maybe the water from your eyes will do the trick.
- Wear a beeper so he can page you from the sandbox or wherever he is when he has to go potty.
- Learn to read body language.
- Give the baby-sitter a bonus if she brings training in ahead of schedule.
- If he isn't trained by four lie about his age.

As with every part of child training there are some no-no's. The following are a few:

- Don't explain to the clerk when you buy diapers why she isn't trained yet.
- Don't read him the entry in the baby book saying his sister was trained at 18 months.
- Don't threaten to cut her out of your will if she doesn't go on the potty.
- Don't make other family members use the restroom at the gas station.
- Don't ever run out of enthusiasm for complimenting him when he tells you he has gone to the bathroom. Never, ever say, "Big deal!"
- Don't make the praise so sweet he'll be calling you from school to report he has gone to the bathroom.

Potty training takes over your life. You can get so caught up in it that when your husband comes out of the bathroom you will say to him, "Good boy!"

Chapter 7

There is no Substitute for Bed

When he calls out to you for water
You tell him no child died of thirst
But he will not be placated
He responds, "I could be the first!"

Nap time is a sneak preview of bedtime and whets your appetite for the real thing. The American dream is having the children go off to bed an hour after supper the first time you say, "Time for bed".

Going to bed is good for the child and it's good for you. It is twice blessed. It is your one shot at getting something done such as reports for work, cleaning, studying or relaxing.

An adult is wise enough to think of sleep as body repair but the child thinks it is something destructive and demoralizing. They feel it is detention.

They act like every night is New Year's Eve and they want to see the New Year in.

They always plead not tired. Do they think the parent is going to say, "Oh, well then forget it?"

26

You've given them their de-caffeinated Ovaltine and they start their stalling tactics.

- He gets terribly interested in the President's State of the Union message.

- He says, "The man on TV told us to stay tuned".

- He says he has to rotate the tires on his toy cars.

- She takes the long scenic route to her bedroom.

- He God blesses kids he hates.

- She God blesses everybody that was at the family reunion.

While you have something to lure the child out of bed in the morning like Krispie Krunchies you have nothing to lure him into bed at night.

***Getting children to bed is a worthwhile
but difficult task.***

Putting the kids to bed is a misnomer. You have to get them to go to bed. You must work hard at selling bed to them. The following are a few suggestions to get the child to buy bed.

- Pretend he is going to the moon and his bed is a space station.

- Make her juices flow. Say, "The bed is so soft"… "The sheets are so fresh"… "I'll fluff your pillow"… "Shut out the rest of the world".

- Write jingles about bed such as:

  Mr. Bed is a wonderful friend.
  He makes it fun to see the day end.

  Violets are blue, roses are red.
  I love Mommy and Daddy and also bed.

- Frequently re-decorate their bedrooms so it has a new look. This could help for a night or two to get them into it.

- Draw pictures of children yawning to show them.

- Start the search for the beloved stuffed animal or blanket well before bedtime.

- Don't let them get a popsicle or anything out of the freezer. The cold blast of air will make them more wide awake.

- Create a contest. Have them write 25 words or less why they like to go to bed.

- Bet them they can't somersault all the way to their bedrooms. If their bedrooms are upstairs use "run upstairs backward" or "walk upstairs on your hands".

- Tell them their stuffed animals are getting lonesome for them.

- Have a sleepathon. Tell them you'll give them a penny for every minute they sleep between 7:00 and 8:00 PM.

- Keep the drapes drawn all day so you can lie about the time.

- Say, "Let's rehearse going to bed." Then say, "That's a take. Cut!"

- Hire an expensive baby-sitter and hang around to see how she gets them to bed.

There are blanket clips but not child clips so it is impossible to get children to stay in bed after you've shed blood, sweat and tears accomplishing the difficult feat of getting them there.

They are always ready with an excuse when you say, "What are you doing out here?" One kid said, "Somebody was trying to get into my wall safe" and he didn't even have a piggy bank.

You can live in the middle of Manhatten and they'll hear lions and coyotes.

Other samples of ridiculous excuses are:

- "I got a wake-up call."

- "Somebody waxed my bed."

Although a child who went to bed and stayed there two consecutive nights would make the Guiness Book of Records there are some things that could be done to better the situation:

- Learn to lip read so you can have the sound off TV.

- Do a bed check only when you're absolutely sure they're asleep.

- If one child wants the light on and one wants it off leave it on and put sunglasses on the other one.

- Say, "I won't let it get back to your friends that you went to bed and stayed there."

- Don't let them look at a catalogue. They'll keep running out to show you things they want.

While you know it would never be possible to call a delivery service and say, "I have a child I want you to deliver to bed" it does seem that getting kids to go night-night is a field that could be further explored. Two things that could help get children to sleep are:

- Rockers on children's beds.

- A toll-free number to dial so the child could hear a lullabye.

For the benefit of the child there could be camouflage P.J.'s so they could rejoin the parents in the living room and not be seen.

Chapter 8

Mothers are Dirt Busters

*Wouldn't it be wonderful
If when you bathed them after play
Kids were like a carpet
And there was dirt-resistant spray?*

Part of the scheduled maintenance of a child is the bath.

Even if you had a course in bathing the baby in your pre-natal classes and the teacher told you that you did very well don't be cocky. Squirming, stiffening and screaming are the chief problems and an inanimate doll doesn't do any of these things.

"I gave the baby his bath" is a common statement as if it's a foregone conclusion that the baby will receive a bath daily.

Even in the olden times the baby wasn't one of the family members who only received a bath on Saturday night. Each morning at 10:00 the oven door would be opened so the heat would keep the baby warm while he was unclothed and the bath was administered.

Why does the baby have to have a general bath every single day? You do spot bathing every time you change him and feed him. Unless the person holding the baby has dirty hands how can the baby get dirty? Do you feel a week-old baby will suddenly start talking and say to a visitor "My mother didn't give me a bath yesterday."

31

***No matter how much the child pleads, stuffed animals
should not be used as bathtub toys.***

A baby doesn't need a bath every single day. You may
occasionally skip a day.

It is easier to get the bath in when the child is portable. When
he begins to walk you must round him up. No matter how dirty
he gets he will not turn himself in. If you live in a new house
where the lawn and sidewalk are pending, the dirt will be
inflated. By night your child will look like a miniature bum.

Dirt can't be erased. It can't be vacuumed off. Soap and water
applied within a bathtub is the only answer.

You must remember that a kid is not bad just because he
doesn't want to take a bath. Also that keeping clean is not a
matter of self-discipline. Getting dirty was not pre-meditated; it
just happened. Therefore when you are bathing him attack the
dirt and not the child.

Have pleasant conversations with your children about taking a
bath. Say, "Who are you?" When he says, "Nicky Smith," say
"You aren't the Nicky Smith I know. The Nicky Smith I know
doesn't have a dirty face and grimy hands and greasy hair."

Negative dialogue does not make bath time something to look forward to. For instance don't say, "You got those hard-to-scrub elbows from your father's side of the family."

As with everything else there is talent in giving baths. With a talented bather a speck of grime is never seen on the child after he gets out of the tub.

If you are devoid of bathing talent learn to make excuses like "He has an ear problem so I can't thoroughly scrub his ears."

Even though you lack skill in this area there are things you can do to improve matters:

- If the children are small enough there can be concurrent bathing. However be sure to notice when they are too old for this and you should go to consecutive baths. Put marks on the floor of the tub and watch for bottoms extending over the marks.

- Bargain with him to get him into the tub. Tell him you'll wash just his ears, his left arm and his right leg.

- Wear waterproof attire. It is impossible to jump out of the way fast from a kneeling position.

- Put a lot of soap on the wash cloth. Let the soap do the work instead of you.

- When you bathe more than one child at a time there will be a power struggle for items in the tub such as a rubber duck or a bar of soap. Therefore have more than one of each item.

- Wear a captain's hat while you bathe him, have boats in the water and sing, "Anchor's Away".

- Put on an exercise tape and bathe them with rhythm.

- Even if you have a ceiling fan in the bathroom you still have to dry them with a towel.

- No matter how much the child pleads stuffed animals should not be used as bathtub toys.

- You can't give half a bath, go rest, then finish it later.

- If you want to get out of giving a bath feed them a lunch right before bedtime and say they shouldn't go into the water so soon after eating.

A clean child is necessary to have the reputation of being a good mother. Fortunately there is no way to tell how long the dirt has been on the child so you can always act as if it is only minutes old.

Chapter 9

We Need a Mopper in Aisle 4

When the Manager asks of you,
"Are you sure that you must shop?"
Show a picture of empty cupboards
So he won't make you stop.

You can't eat every meal at a drive-in so you will have to go grocery shopping.

With the high price of groceries you certainly do not want to add the cost of a baby-sitter to it so therefore you will bring your children with you to the supermarket.

This can get so bad you will imagine that next time you go there will be bouncers. But remember it is easier than taking kids out into the wilderness to get food where our early ancestors had to go to get it.

There are many things to do that can help you in the venture of grocery shopping with kids.

If a neighbor asks you to pick up a few things for her, try to deal; you'll do it if she keeps your kids while you're getting them. However you will be lucky of this works even once. Of course she will never ask you again.

The best thing is to do as good a job as you can with them accompanying you. Here are some tips:

- Try to get your child to nap in the cart. You can use a roll of paper toweling for a pillow.
- If one child hits the other in the eye use one of your frozen items to put on the eye.
- Ask the person selling poppies outside the store if your child can help him sell.
- Give him the job of untangling carts for other shoppers.
- If possible find a cart with wheels that need oiling. It will help drown out your kids.
- Skip the items that are optional in the recipe.
- Buy Generic products. Kids aren't as eager to get into them.
- Put your child on the floor of the cart under the basket. There won't be much head room but he won't be able to grab items off the shelves.

Don't let him hitchhike a ride in someone else's cart.

- Dress your kids in inconspicuous clothing. When they keep running back for samples they won't be as noticeable.
- Bring along Scotch tape to repair packages that your kids wreck.
- Have a notebook to write down prices of items as you buy them. If your child has torn off the price you don't want to hold up the line while the cost is checked.
- At the check-out loudly mention a gossip item from a tabloid to take away attention from your kids.

There are certain things that you should avoid while getting provisions for the family so the expedition will not be a worse disaster.

- Don't go down the diaper aisle with a recently trained child. He will immediately say he has to go potty.
- Don't go down the pet food aisle if you don't have a pet. They will start begging for one.
- Don't let your kids play games with carts — such as Aiming for Shoppers' Heels.
- Don't pay by check. You can be traced if damage is discovered.
- Don't let them hitchhike a ride in someone else's cart.

It is better not to expect grocery shopping to be enjoyable. The following are a few grocery shopping unpleasantries you can look forward to:

- Your kids will fight over who will hand the money to the checker.
- The checker will give you a no-wonder-they-act-like-they-do look as she rings up candy and cookies.
- In looking at items in the clearance cart you are apt to see items your child wrecked on your last trip.

If supermarket owners had the sympathy they should have for mothers shopping with children they would put TVs with cartoon videos in the carts.

Try to be patient with your children. What if Isaac Newton's mother had screamed at him when an apple fell?!

Chapter 10

There's More to Leave than What's in the Will

Cars become outdated
Clothes of yesteryear seem strange
But what mothers say to children
Somehow will never change.

Although children definitely do not give mothers the feeling they are talking for posterity it seems mothers are really doing that.

Mothers may have their individual style but the same words that were said by a mother are said by her daughter when she becomes a mother.

The following are some samples of things mothers say while raising their children:

- "You'll thank me later."
- "Don't tease your sister."
- "You call that a haircut?!"
- "Don't run with the scissors."
- "It would be nice to have a little help around here."
- "Stop making a nuisance of yourself."
- "Don't talk with your mouth full."
- "Don't chew with your mouth open."
- "Now, apologize to your sister."

Maybe mothers' voices should have amplifiers.

- "Never mind, I'll do it myself!"
- "If I have to pull this car over ..."
- "You'll never get into a good college if you don't study."
- "Remember it's a school night."
- "Is that asking too much?"
- "You're too quiet. What are you up to in there?"
- "Don't run in the house!"
- "I want an explanation of what's going on here."
- "How many times do I have to tell you?"
- "I want to talk to you."
- "Don't get smart with me!"
- "You heard me!"
- "Get back here!"
- "Who do you think you're kidding?"
- "Be quiet! — Do you want the neighbors to hear?"
- "I wouldn't wear that to a dog fight!"

- "Put down that stick! You could poke your eye out!"
- "Just because her mother lets **her** do it don't think I'm going to let **you** do it."
- "I said 'no' and I mean 'no'."
- "I'm counting to ten ..."
- "I'll give you **something** to **cry** about."
- "This hurts me more than it hurts you."
- "You're old enough to know better."
- "If you don't come now I'm leaving you here."
- "Now get to sleep — you have a big day ahead."
- "Does anyone have to go potty?"
- "Now don't be a pest."
- "Some day you'll know what it's like to be a mother."
- "This is the last time we're going to take a vacation together."
- "Don't put it on your plate if you aren't going to eat it."
- "One day you'll be sorry and then it'll be too late."
- "Will somebody get the phone?"
- "Don't sit too close to the TV."
- "So long as you're living under this roof you'll abide by my rules."
- "What is there to do out there after midnight?"
- "You never learned that in this house!"
- "Do you think I'm made of money?"
- "I suppose you call that fun."
- "You act like you've got stock in the phone company."
- "I just don't know what to think about you."
- "Look where you're walking."
- "Can't you be quiet during the news?"
- "I'm not bluffing."

- "Why do you always wait until the last minute to do anything?"

- "C is average. Are you willing to settle for average?"

- "Get along!"

- "You need a little cracking down on."

- "It isn't going to hurt you to take your little brother along."

- "He'll admire you for saying 'no'."

- "We'll just see about that."

- "Come with me, young lady!"

- "If he jumped off a cliff would you jump off a cliff?"

- "Were you raised in a barn?"

- "Maybe next time you'll listen to me!"

- "Hurry up! You'll make us all late!"

- "Call me when you get there."

- "No, there aren't any onions in there."

- "You're giving up a good job — with benefits?!!"

- "You're not too big to hit."

- "You don't have to listen, but I'm going to say this."

Chapter 11
Get Your Mind
Out of the Clutter

Kids won't help with cleaning
If you grab them by their collars
Say, "Maybe you'll find a comic book
That is worth a thousand dollars."

Housework can be murder when you have children. Right after you have cleaned and straightened everything disarray returns. Nine-tenths of the time your house will have a burglary-scene look.

You will go through stages before you adjust to a messy house. First there will be denial, then anger and finally acceptance.

A child's room is always a sore point with a mother. The following are some reported statements about messy kids' rooms:

- "He's a kicker on the football team so he's good at kicking his clothes out of the way to make a path."

- "If it were a ship they would scuttle it."

- "I sent him to the hall because he couldn't get into his room."

- "I was encouraged when she took 10 dust cloths to her room but she tied them together and escaped out the window."

- "He thinks hangers are only for opening locked car doors."

- "You wouldn't think dust could settle the way her room shakes from her music."

- "She stopped to use an emery board on her nails 10 times while she was cleaning."
- "There are even clothes thrown on top of the canopy over her bed."
- "The only time her floor gets swept is when she breaks a glass."
- "She wants a mirrored ceiling so she can locate lost items."

When it comes to cleaning children do not want to get involved. They think the only purpose of the broom closet is to play hide and seek.

One child sent his chore list to his grandmother for sympathy.

Kids are very good at coming up with excuses for not helping you clean. The following are a few examples:

- "Clean windows encourage window peepers."
- "If I'm vacuuming I won't be able to hear the phone."

IT'S 7:00 — DO YOU KNOW WHERE YOUR DOLLS ARE?

Tell them their dolls and toy soldiers have a curfew — they have to be in the toy box by 7:00 PM.

- "I have scrubber's elbow."
- "I can't clean because my goal is to become a hand model."
- "Cleaning chemicals burn my eyes."

You can't expect children to volunteer to help you with the job of cleaning the house, but if you put some fun into it you may be able to get a little work out of them. Some suggestions are:

- Tell them their dolls and toy soldiers have a curfew — they have to be in the toy box by 7:00 PM.
- Put a horn on your vacuum sweeper.
- Have a tie-dyed bag on the sweeper.
- Have designer dust cloths.
- Make them name tags as if they're a professional cleaning service.
- Get them to hang things up by saying, "Honor thy blouse and thy skirt."
- Let them have specialties like the bathroom faucets.
- Provide music such as "Whistle While you Work," "This is the way we Scrub a House," or "Rocky's" theme song.

Putting off housework till the kids grow up is not the answer. Tricking people into thinking you're a better housekeeper than you are is. The following are a few ideas:

- Put a lemon in a bowl of fruit. It smells like you've been dusting.
- Say that you're trying to increase your home's livability.
- Tell guests the dust on the top of your grandfather clock is there to represent gray hair.
- If there's milk sitting out on the table say that you're getting it to room temperature for a recipe.
- Put a decal on your glass patio door. It will make it seem that you keep it so clean there is danger of people trying to walk through it.
- Vacuum your throw rugs before you shake them outside.
- Leave a boarding pass in sight. It gives the impression you have been travelling and weren't home to clean.
- If you have a dirty sofa pillow throw it on the floor when the doorbell rings. People will assume it belongs to a cat or dog.
- For a dirty carpet yell upstairs, "Who's tracking?!"

Be sure you don't take pictures inside the house to send to your mother-in-law.

Chapter 12

In Sickness and in Health you Have to Take your Child to a Pediatrician

Before you say, "He's got tremors
His whole body seems to shake,"
Check his Rock 'n Roll music
That could cause the earth to quake.

You can't provide protection for your child against bullies but you can provide protection for him against whooping cough, diptheria, measles and polio. A good mother has a close relationship with a pediatrician.

Usually the pediatrician tells you to bring your baby in when he is six weeks' old, when he is six months' old and then he'll say, "Bring him in when he's a year". (However don't expect birthday balloons on this visit.)

Some mothers interview pediatricians before they select one. Others just look to see how healthy the doctor's children look in the photo on his desk.

There will be times between regular check-ups when you will have to take your child to the doctor. However, often you will not be sure whether it is necessary to consult a physician. The following are a couple of signals that will tell you that you should:

- You haven't recently said, "Sit down, you're blocking TV."

- You haven't recently said, "Don't throw the ball in the house."

Feed your child healthy food before the
appointment so when the pediatrician asks
him what he's been eating it sounds good.

Don't think pain is persisting just because it lasts 15 minutes.

A mother can make anything sound bad. You must be careful your motherly concern doesn't cause you to say something that will give the doctor a false picture. An example would be saying, "He has night sweats" when he tussles with his dog before bedtime.

The following are some suggestions for handling your role as as mother taking a child to a pediatrician:

- Make appointments so they fall before his birthday or Christmas so you can threaten no presents if he doesn't behave.

- Dress your child in a turtle neck so you can pull it over his mouth and nose if there are children coughing in the waiting room.

- Feed your child healthy food before the appointment so when the pediatrician asks him what he's been eating it sounds good.

- Wash his arms thoroughly. It is embarrassing if the alcohol-moistened cotton swab turns black.

- Sit in the chair in the waiting room that is furthest from the doctor's office. In case someone cries in there it will be less audible.

- Bring your baby book along with you to the pediatrician and fill it in in front of him.

- Have another patient in the waiting room ask some of your questions if the list is over a page.

- Let your child take some of his toys along with him to the doctor's office, but not his big wheel.

You can't stand at the door of the waiting room and ask, "Which ones are here for check-ups and which ones are here because they're sick" so you'll know where to sit. There are other no-no's regarding your child and the pediatrician:

- Don't have your child think there is anything unpleasant about the visit, such as saying, "This shot can take the place of your next spanking."

- Don't make the doctor come and see how well your child is playing with the other children in the waiting room.

- It's all right for your child to go through your purse while you're in the waiting room but don't let her continue on and go through the doctor's black bag.

- Don't hug your child hard and kiss him as the nurse takes him into another room to be weighed.

47

- Don't ask silly questions such as, "Is it true a little bit of sugar makes the medicine go down?"

- Don't ask your doctor to put a tarp over his equipment so your child won't be scared.

You haven't done a good job of preparing your child to go to the pediatrician if it takes you and the doctor and his nurse to pull your child's thumb from his mouth so the doctor can look at his throat.

Chapter 13

No, we Can't Take the Tree and Tree House With Us

Don't expect for a minute
It will ward off a sob
If you say, "Children, dear,
It's a much better job."

We are a mobile society so moving will probably be part of your life. It is very conceivable that some night your husband will greet you with the news that his company is transferring him.

A good wife accepts this news pleasantly. She doesn't stall for time by saying something like, "I want to hear it from the boss himself".

However, moving is more difficult when you have children. They imagine the new neighbors will be Martians and the new kids at school will be The Dead End Kids. A signal they don't want to move is if they egg your FOR SALE sign.

The week after you move your kids will feel like they're in isolation. Therefore you must put a lot of thought into the re-location.

- First make them think you are moving to some remote place like Yugoslavia. They'll be relieved when they find out they will be much closer to their old home than they thought they'd be.

49

- Tell them they shouldn't hold back from crying. Crying is preferable to slamming doors and saying nasty things.

- Watch reruns of The Little House on the Prairie. They will realize how lucky they are.

- Tell them, "It's not like we're moving some place where there isn't a McDonald's."

Kids having to move act like they're being kidnapped — and they would probably like to impose the same punishment on you that kidnappers get.

While you can't expect them to kiss the ground when they get to the new house you can do some things that will make it possible to live with them:

- Work with a realtor who has promised to convince your children moving is a good idea.

- Give them both quality **and** quantity time.

*Rent Big Bird and ask the new neighbors
if they will pretend he lives with them.*

- If you get your child a dog to make up for the friends he left make sure it goes to dog obedience school. You don't want to be known as "that new family with the terrible dog".

- Have the TV hooked up before the washer and dryer. They'd rather be dirty than not have TV.

- Let them know they can still stay in touch with their old friends. Promise them you'll get an 800 number.

- Buy moving-day sweat bands in the colors of their new school.

- Rent Big Bird and ask the new neighbors if they will pretend he lives with them.

- Tell him he has to be nice to the new kids. They won't provide police protection for him in the new neighborhood.

There are some things you should avoid:

- Don't let them hear the theme song of Cheers — "You want to go some place where everybody knows your name."

- Don't object to digging up the turtle they have buried in the back yard.

- Be very careful you don't forget one of the kids when you stop at a Wayside while driving to your new home. He will feel even more insecure.

However, whatever you do or don't do, moving will break the mood of one big happy family.

Chapter 14

Is There a Camp Counselor in the House?

To control your children
Only makes sense
If at the next campsite
They're building a fence.

Do you hate camping so much the only place you want to pitch the tent is through the store window where your husband bought it?

There are so many wonderful things about camping that you should not let the negatives keep you from enjoying this family adventure.

It must be fun. Otherwise as you drive into a campground you would see people scalping stickers.

Pleasant aspects of camping are beautiful views, cooking over a fire, eating outdoors, having the moon and stars overhead, finding berries and viewing countless blessings of nature close-up.

Other pleasantries are:

- There are no bellboys to tip.

- Kids can't slam a tent door.

- Your child will be "new kid on the block" in only a matter of minutes.

Don't buy insect repellent for your children.
Scratching keeps them busy.

- Bad-tasting camp water keeps them from asking for drinks after they are in bed.

- Your reflection in the lake is flattering.

However there are things that could put a crimp in camping. For instance your kids will loudly complain they are missing their favorite TV shows. Bringing along the TV Guide so they can read a synopsis of it won't help.

Also you'll have a stiff neck from looking at the sky to see if it's going to rain.

The following are some suggestions that could make you a happier camper:

- Pick a good campsite. A good campsite is one that is within five minutes of a motel in case it storms.

- Take a direct route, not a scenic route, to the campground. It's better to enjoy the scenery when the kids are out of the car.

- Write down the names of motels with VACANCY signs as you get close to your destination.

- Drive around until you find a family with extremely rowdy kids and take the site next to them. Your kids won't seem as bad.

- Keep the food up high in trees out of reach of bears and your kids.

- Bring along forks to roast marshmallows so they won't say, "Your stick is longer than mine."

- If you run out of clean clothes for your children put their dirty ones on inside out and say they dressed themselves.

- Leave a mint on their sleeping bag so they won't miss staying at a motel.

Your husband will busy himself putting up the tent, building the fire, and reading maps so you will be left to take care of the children.

When they want to go home nothing can change their minds. Therefore you should think of entertainment for them so they'll want to stay — at least as long as it took to put up the tent. The following are some ideas:

- Have them name their mosquito bites.

- Make them blow up their own air mattresses. It saps a little of their energy.

- Give a prize to the one who untangles the most fish lines.

- Suggest they take a hike and look for coins to use in the computer games when you go to town. Plant several coins along the path.

- Have them have a marshmallow fight.

- Get them to become bird, butterfly, bug and turtle watchers.

Statements during a camping expedition will not be just "Isn't it glorious" and "This is the way to live" exclamations. The following is some more common camp conversation:

- "I know you can't sleep with the light on but I can't do anything about the stars."

- "Think of removing burrs from your legs as shaving them."

- "I realize the crickets are keeping you awake but I wouldn't know where to start to kill them all."

- "You are not going to just sit out in the car 'til we're ready to go home."

- "There is no way a telephone can be installed at a campsite for three days."

There are some things to avoid in your quest to have a happy experience living in the outdoors:

- Don't buy insect repellent for your children. Scratching keeps them busy.

- Don't let your son bring his amplifiers for around the campfire singing.

- Don't try to teach anyone under two how to read a compass. Watch them so they don't wander away.

- Don't let them put a sign in the camp office for a ride home.

- Don't use every pan for drips. Save one or two for cooking.

- Don't bring along heirloom quilts.

- Don't have camp songs be TV theme songs.

If it rained all the time you were camping don't picket the TV station that predicted fair weather.

Chapter 15

Birthday Parties Should Be Considered Unlawful Assemblage

If you have a party
For your child who is five
Don't expect to have fun
Just try to survive.

Every 30 seconds in America a birthday party is given.

A birthday party is an event where the kid who is tardy for school every day arrives an hour early and where the kid who never speaks above a whisper shouts at the top of his lungs all afternoon.

Adults wouldn't be that rowdy if there were a two-hour open bar.

But part of being a parent is inviting friends of your child to help him celebrate his birthday. You don't want your offspring to someday be lying on a psychiatrist's couch saying he never had a birthday party and the psychiatrist telling him that is the reason he is having difficulty with life.

Remember that the next celebration will be a wedding and everything you suggest in planning that will be vetoed. You are the executive producer of the birthday party.

There are things you should do beforehand:

- Get a stress test to see if you are up to having the party.

- Buy liniment for the day after the party.

- That morning apply extra deodorant.

- Increase your tranquilizer dosage.

- Find someone who hauls away debris cheap.

If you had put on the invitations that the refreshments were going to be liver and onions every kid would show up. In fact don't be surprised if you send out 15 invitations and receive 50 R.S.V.P.'s saying they'll be there.

Unfortunately you can't ask that the invitee provide references. You must take your chances.

If your son says he can't ask certain kids because they're not speaking to each other invite them. It might result in the party being a teeny bit quieter.

Give the party during your lunch hour.

An adult will put a lampshade on his head at a party; a child will break a lamp.

There are many acts of desperation that will pop into your mind to get you through the worst afternoon of your life but usually they must be rejected. The following are a few samples:

- Write on the invitations, "Bring along homework."
- Write "sharp" after the ending time of the party.
- Give the party during your lunch hour.
- Hire a hypnotist to keep them under a spell during the party.
- Snap the rubber band holding on the birthday hat of an obnoxious kid.
- When playing Blind Man's Bluff twirl the obnoxious kid around so many times he gets sick and has to go home.
- Threaten, "My people will take care of you."
- Send the kids home in the middle of the night from a birthday slumber party because it's no longer your kid's birthday.
- Have the water turned off so there won't be balloon water fights.
- Take back your kid's presents to pay for the damages.

The following are a few suggestions to help with the trauma of a birthday party:

- To avoid cleaning your house beforehand call it Batman's Cave.
- Plan games. You can't say to five-year olds, "Just mingle."
- Have in view pictures of a kid running and of a kid jumping on a bed with red diagonal lines through them.
- If the weather is bad and the party has to be held indoors insist there must be a fire drill so you will get them out of the house for a little while.

- Provide a brand new handkerchief for blindfold games. A kid may point out his daddy's handkerchiefs are a lot whiter.

- Sing multiple verses of "Happy Birthday" like "How old are you?" "How many sisters have you?" "How many brothers have you?" They stay out of trouble while they're singing "Happy Birthday."

- Tell your child he has to keep silent while opening his gifts in order to get his wish. This will keep him from saying, "I've already got one of these."

- Five-year olds don't ooh and aah over an ice sculpture so save your money.

- If you run out of prizes see if you have an unopened box of cereal with a toy.

- Have only one flavor of ice cream. If they see somebody else with another flavor they'll want that one.

- Make sure the party is still going on when your husband gets home from work so he'll know what you went through.

- Arrange to return the kids to their homes yourself. Parents show up late.

There are certain things a mother giving a birthday party must expect:

- You'll have to make at least one peanut butter sandwich.

- There will be a fight in the food line.

- Nobody will want to sit by the Birthday Boy's mom.

- You won't be able to get the words "Come again" out of your mouth.

If you decide to have the party at a restaurant don't pick your favorite because you won't be able to show up there for a long time.

Chapter 16

Why Don't They Make Belated Thank-You Cards?

They receive many a gift
About which they're ecstatic
But they delay writing "Thank You"
'Til the gift's in the attic.

You will get to the point where you hope your child will never receive another gift as long as he lives. This is because one of the hardest tasks a mother faces is getting her son or daughter to write a thank-you note.

There will be a lot of conversation between you and your child about the need for him to express his gratitude for a present, such as:

Child: They'll know I'm grateful.

Mother: Not unless you tell them.

Child: How can they be that stupid?!

Samples of a child's comments on the thank-you note:

- "I'm sure they got it on sale — can I write a shorter thank-you note?"

- "Well, will they send me a thank-you note for my thank-you note?"

***Make him buy his own stamps and tell him
the price of stamps is going up.***

- "Can I say, 'Thank you for this gift and any future gifts you may give me?'"
- "I know why it's better to give than to receive — you don't have to write a thank-you note."
- "If I thanked her twice over the phone would that take the place of a written thank you?"

When you meet the giver of the gift you will feel you have to make excuses for the delay of the note.

You can't blame slow mail for more than three weeks. The following are a few suggestions of things to say that will make you feel better even though they won't necessarily make the giver think more kindly of your child:

- "My son had the thank-you note in his shirt pocket and I washed it."
- "As soon as my son learns to spell better he's going to write you."

- "My daughter is planning to take a course in calligraphy and she's waiting until she completes it to write her thank-you's."

- "She's not going to send you a thank-you note but she's going to name her first child after you."

- "My son's thank-you note to you is in its final draft."

- "You'll be getting that thank you as soon as that clumsy cast gets off."

- "As soon as the shock of getting such a magnificent present wears off he'll write you."

Only a very rude person would respond, "Are you sure he isn't waiting for a stamp with his head on it to come out?"

It would be nice if the person giving the gift wrote on the card accompanying it, "Please omit thank-you note" but since this never happens you must prod your child to get to the necessary correspondence. The following are a few suggestions:

- Keep bringing up the gift and raving about it.

- Don't let him use the gift until he writes a thank you.

- This won't work if it's an ugly necktie.

- Place the address book in the refrigerator.

- Make him buy his own stamps and tell him the price of stamps is going up.

- Say, "I'm going to the Post Office. Do you have any thank-you notes you want me to mail?"

- Ask, "Why doesn't one of your graduation parties be a Writing Thank-You Notes party?"

- Tell him to put "Write Thank-You's" on his list of things to do. If he doesn't have a list of things to do write "Nag son to write thank-you's" on your list.

A few more hints about the thank-you's:

- Be sure the note you wrote for your child to copy does not accidentally get in the envelope with his note.

- Don't send a "Thank-you note will be forthcoming" note.

- Don't edit his note. Just be glad he wrote it. People are very tolerant of starter thank-you notes.

If you get really desperate dial the person's number and hand your child the phone or have a thank you published in the newspaper.

Chapter 17

All I Want for Christmas is her Two Front Teeth to Come in Straight

You must be prepared to hear the news,
"Your daughter will have to wear braces,"
Unless you move her to Africa
Where veils cover women's faces.

The thought of having your child go to an orthodontist could cancel the thrill of the words, "He's got a tooth!"

Haven't you ever wondered when the first braces were used and when the percentage of children wearing them went up to 99%?

There should be more variables in mouths so orthodontia wouldn't be needed so frequently.

When a baby is ignoring Rock-a-bye Baby and then finally stops crying by putting his thumb in his mouth, don't enjoy the peace — worry about protruding teeth. Pull the thumb out of his mouth and tell yourself you are earning money by listening to him cry.

The following are a couple more suggestions regarding orthodontia:

- Put his retainer in your wall safe when he's not wearing it.

- Have a picture on your desk of your child smiling her pre-orthodontia smile. It will make you realize why you're working.

The no-no's are:

- Don't start an envelope at work to help pay the orthodontists's bill.

- Don't count the time driving to and from the orthodontist and waiting for your child's turn. Just count the time he is in the chair when you figure time spent on getting teeth straightened.

- Don't tell yourself crooked teeth will keep her humble and forget the orthodontia.

One good thing is that teeth are never hopeless. You may have to take out second and third mortgages on your house, car and boat, but any mouth can be landscaped to be good looking.

One bad thing is there are no hand-me-down braces.

With all this money put into straightening teeth you must make sure proper care is given them. (One mother said her son brushed so seldom she found herself checking to see if there was an expiration date on his toothpaste.)

One bad thing is there are no hand-me-down braces.

However don't go so far as the mother who had her daughter use a toothbrush blessed by the Pope.

The following are a few suggestions to make sure these beautiful teeth last:

- Set the table with a toothbrush next to the spoon so they remember to brush after every meal.

- Wear a THANK YOU FOR BRUSHING pin.

- Tell him he'll whistle better if he brushes his teeth well.

- Have the tooth fairy leave a toothbrush along with money under the pillow. (A toothbrush without money would be upsetting.)

- Call the City Water Department to make sure the flouride level is what it should be.

- Promote peace among your children so he doesn't get punched in the mouth.

His or her attractive smile is your reward. Unfortunately they do not choose to reward you frequently.

Chapter 18

Mrs. Jones are you Listening? I Was Talking About your Son's Attention Span

You feel the teacher is going to ask,
"If we skip him a grade, would you mind?"
But that isn't what she wants at all —
She says, "I think I'll keep him behind."

Teachers' conferences make a good case for teaching your child at home. I'm sure even Mrs. Einstein was shaken when Albert brought home a notice that teachers' conferences were coming up. You never know what you're going to be told.

No matter how successful you are in the business world this is not a case of saying, "My people will call your people." You must sit in that chair beside the teacher's desk and listen to what she has to say about your child.

Another impossible solution to get you out of this ordeal is sending a video tape saying, "I'm sorry I can't be with you tonight ..."

While you cannot escape the conference there are some things you can do to make it easier. The following are a few suggestions:

- Arrange an early morning conference so you aren't fully awake and all of what she says doesn't sink in.

THIS IS KEN'S GRANDMOTHER AND SHE WANTS TO HEAR WHAT YOU HAVE TO SAY ABOUT HIM.

**Bring along your mother or mother-in-law.
There's a chance the teacher will say less
terrible things in front of his grandmother.**

- Go to the conference with an unruly toddler whether he belongs to you or someone else. The teacher will hurry with you.

- Plop your child's most angelic-looking picture on the teacher's desk while you are discussing him.

- Bring along your mother or mother-in-law. There's a chance the teacher will say less terrible things in front of his grandmother.

- Oooh and aaah about her bulletin boards.

- Sit on the edge of the chair as if you're extremely interested in your child's progress.

- Dress dowdy. She may feel sorry for you and feel she can't add another burden.

- Bring along a box of kleenex. It could make her afraid that she will make you cry.

- If you see a mother whose child is a terror insist she go ahead of you. Your child's antics will seem better in comparison.

- Try to keep your child out of the conversation as much as possible by asking her about her vacation... where she went to college, etc.

- Hang around and eavesdrop on other conferences. She may be that rough on all kids.

There are also some stunts you could pull that would make the conference worse. The following are some things you can't say at teachers' conferences:

- "Hasn't anybody ever taught you that if you can't say anything good about somebody you shouldn't say anything."

- "I wouldn't talk that way about your child."

- "Gossip is not my forte."

- "That's a cheap shot."

- "Lies! lies! All of it's lies!!"

- "If you're going to be outspoken, "I'm going to be outspoken too. He doesn't like you."

- "Teachers of the Year say only good things to parents about their children."

- "Aren't you being a little picky?"

- "Could we take a break and start in again in about 10 minutes?"

It is very important that you weigh every word you say. It's not going to help your child's cause to tell the teacher he learned to tie his shoelaces at 3½.

- When the teacher gives a general criticism such as, "He's naughty" or "He's lazy" don't ask for an example. She'll give you one.

- If she says, "He lies" don't ask her to please change that to "He tells stories."

- Don't get a second opinion from his substitute teacher. It would probably be worse.

- Don't ask for dirt on some other kid.

There are also **actions** that could be detrimental:

- Don't knit during conferences.

- Don't dig your fingernails into the palm of your hand so hard it bleeds and you have to go to the school nurse.

- Don't slam the door on your way out.

While waiting for the conference tell yourself if it were really bad she'd have asked to see both parents.

Chapter 19

Don't Discipline When There Are Only Five Shopping Days Left 'Til Mother's Day

You must keep your child from wrong —
If it's his biting everyone's afraid of
Don't use the "Bite 'Em Back" cure
Say, "Spinach is what people are made of."

You can't divorce your child — you have to shape him up so you can live with him.

Parents must face the fact that most children have the chronic illness "Naughtiness." This is hard to do as it is so much easier to think that your child is perfect. Therefore it is a good idea to have a list of signals that will tip you off that your child has flaws and even though he doesn't have a record with the police he does have one with teachers and neighbors:

- He gets extra credit for being absent.

- Neighbors always have their cement poured while you are on vacation.

- You often find the phone off the hook and the mailbox in his room.

71

- You are shopping with your kids and a clerk hands you a flyer from another store.

- Your babysitter tells you she has retired from sitting and is only 12.

- On carload night at the outdoor movies your car gets charged double.

The child who has done something wrong **wants** to be punished. However don't wait until he puts this desire into words before you take action.

The mother most often is the disciplinarian. Even if you are rich you can't have a maid administer a spanking. The father is usually the disciplinarian-elect who never takes office.

It's fun to show a child you love him by buying him toys and candy but it's not fun to show you love him by punishing him.

There are many signals that will tip you off that your child is less than perfect.

Misbehavior can be handled in many different ways but it must be handled and not ignored. Don't expect the problem can be taken care of by saying to the child, "I'm very disappointed in you." You must be sure your child is not discipline deprived.

The following are some suggestions for getting your child to behave:

- You do a better job of disciplining if you're in a bad mood. When your child does something for which he deserves punishment put on shoes that hurt.

- Chew garlic before you deliver a lecture to your son — he will agree with you a lot sooner.

- Threaten to take the cost of your tranquilizers out of his allowance.

- Take a page from today's justice. Have her do so many hours of community service such as raking the lawn or scrubbing the floor.

- Have him write I WILL NOT HIT MY SISTER 500 times. If he does hit her again his arm will be tired and he won't hit her as hard.

- Act like you mean business. This doesn't mean handing her your business card. Use a firm voice and call her by her first, middle and last name. Be careful you don't accidentally use the first and middle name of another one of your children.

- Be melodramatic. Say things like, "I'll leave it to your imagination what I'm going to do if this happens again" or "You're all washed up and you know it!"

- Don't worry if you yell so loud plaster falls down. That might just do the trick.

- Threaten to write to the President and ask him to make his speeches during Sesame Street.

There are many things other than disciplining that you can do about a mischievous child:

- Get outdoor pets such as rabbits and homing pigeons to keep him outside more.

- Volunteer to be on telephone committees so teachers can't get through.

- Go to a church or temple that has a side door so you won't have to walk past the minister, priest or rabbi on the way out.

- Go to PTA meetings. You may get them to lengthen the school day.

- To stop neighbors from coming to you to complain, leave several folded-up newspapers on the front porch and don't answer the door.

- If they phone to complain turn up the volume on the TV and keep saying, "I can't hear you" until they hang up in exasperation.

- If your child carves her initials into a table add two more, carve a heart around them and place it next to a love seat.

- Should she write on a wall, add more writing as if it's planned decorating.

- Tell her to use an alias when she writes in wet cement.

There are also things to avoid in the process of raising your child to be a good adult.

- Don't say, "Any friend of yours is a friend of mine." You'll be surprised at the rotten friends he can dredge up.

- Don't feel giving his crimes publicity is the answer. His friends won't care, his grandparents won't believe it, and it will make your friends too happy.

- Don't point an accusing index finger at him if your fingernail polish is chipped.

- Don't beg your child to behave. This is hard on the knees.

- Don't postpone the punishment:

> Don't say, "Wait till your father gets home" or if you're a single parent, "Wait 'til I get you a father."

> Don't wait until your Ann Landers' letter gets an answer.

> Don't wait until you get in to see your pediatrician.

The discipline works better if you have the backing of the rest of the household — your husband and the other children. It would be ideal if the dog growled and bared his teeth.

Don't be too lenient after a wrong-doing. Remember you cannot re-open the case. The most he will do to retaliate is leave your name out of his prayers that night.

Chapter 20

Her Children are the Perfect Height and Weight for their Ages

Her kids are bathed and asleep
For a treat she bakes cinnamon twist
No wonder numerous sitters ask,
"Pretty please may I be on your list?"

All mothers try to avoid mistakes but Super Mom achieves this goal. Her kids' temperatures never go above 98.6 and their test scores never go below.

Super Mom is so far ahead of the average mother she is demoralizing.

Of course you would make a fool of yourself if you were to confront her and say, "Your being so perfect is making me miserable. Would you mind flubbing up sometimes? I'd really appreciate it." Besides she would probably just deny her fault of perfection.

The best thing you can do is face the wondrous things she does that bother you. The following are some samples of things Super Mom does that cause distress:

- She goes home from the hospital after having a baby in Size 5 jeans.

Mrs. Perfect identifies birds and trees for the children in the carpool on the way to school.

- She has twin girls so she can name them after both grandmothers.

- She circles in the TV Guide all the shows her children are not allowed to watch while she is in the hospital.

- Every day her children look as if they are going to have their school pictures taken.

- She writes all her children's excuses in calligraphy.

- There is never a prescription in the medicine cabinet over a month old.

- She and her sitter synchronize their watches and she is home on the dot.

- Her seat doesn't lop over the little plastic chairs on parents' night.

- She remembers all the names of her children's friends' pets.

- She gets a manicure for cutting her kid's birthday cake.

- She has her children put in deposit slips with the money when they drop it in the piggy bank so they'll be prepared for real banking.

- When she compliments her kids on what they are wearing they just live in that outfit.

- Her daughter goes to the same beauty parlor she does.

- She identifies birds and trees for the children in the carpool on the way to school.

You would think seeing this perfection would bring out the best in you but instead it brings out the worst. It gives you such a feeling of hopelessness that you don't even try.

Watching her shine as a housewife destroys ambition. You know you can never achieve this height of spic and spanness. Therefore you are not the example of domesticity for your daughters that you should be.

The following are some acts of Super Mom that undermine you:

- She uses a legal pad to make her daily chore list.

- She flosses between her piano keys.

- She dusts the inside of her keyholes.

- She sets her mouse traps with miniature cheese trays.

- She makes her own tallies and her own bridge mix.

- Her alphabet soup has Greek letters.

- She has bags printed with her name on them for her rummage sales.

- She puts a rubber mat on the bottom of the bird bath so the birds won't slip.

Naturally Super Mom's children also do things that are upsetting:

- They discuss world events at breakfast.
- By the age of five they can eat with a fork and also chop sticks.
- Her nine-month old can dial 911.
- They have their training wheels taken off their bicycles after riding once to the corner.
- They have never lost a mitten or a glove.
- If there are signs at the zoo that say DO NOT FEED THE ANIMALS her children will not eat in front of the cages.
- They prefer plain apples to taffy apples.
- Her pre-schoolers laugh at political cartoons and can explain them.
- They run the bath water for the next one to take a bath.
- They have never waited for the buzz to remind them to buckle up.
- They give back their allowance if they feel they didn't deserve it.
- After they borrow the car they return it with a full tank of gas.
- They write the due dates of their library books on the calendar.

There is no magic way you can turn into a Super Mom but there are things you can do that will create the illusion you are one:

- Smudge food on your child's flash cards. It will look to the teacher as if you left your cooking to help him with his homework.
- If you have company when your kids are drinking orange pop say, "Watch out for the seeds!"
- Send items to school for Show and Tell in an oatmeal box.

- If you ever **do** give your child a hot breakfast and he gets egg or cream of wheat on his face, **leave it**.

- Even though your kids eat only junk food have a banana peel or orange peel lying on the toy box.

- Have a little girl's apron with flour on it in sight. It will give the impression you are teaching your daughter to bake.

- Say, "I enjoy having my children underfoot" not letting it be known that means you have them play in the basement.

- If you observe someone noticing your child's dirty hands say "He reads every newspaper he can get hold of."

- So guests will be impressed with your discipline serve your child his favorite food and say, "Now you eat every bite of that!"

- Have bookshelves built into the headboard of your baby's bed.

- Always come away from teachers' conferences smiling.

Fortunately cases of Super Moms are rather isolated.

Chapter 21

Post Facts of Life

Children must be told
About the bird and bee
But the years that follow baby
Are not filled with only glee.

Facts of life are told so children will know the results of sexual involvement. However, the facts of life narration ends with the birth of the baby.

The results go on much longer. The following are a few facts that tell what to expect after the children are born:

- It is impossible to enjoy gossip about friends' kids because you know your own are apt to do worse.

- The average adult gets tired playing cards 10 hands before the child gets tired.

- The worry of receiving failure notices makes junk mail thrilling.

- Life isn't fair. If life were fair, kids wouldn't be having their best times while parents are having their worst times.

- Dirt never covers a child so completely that people can't recognize him as yours.

- Cleanliness makes only a cameo appearance in a little boy's life.

- Unbreakable toys take longer to break.

- Medicine is never flavored so well that a child takes it without protest.

- No matter how hard you try, all you'll ever be to an adolescent is one-half of a set of bad parents.

- A crying child can be heard over a parade band.

- By the time you have learned to say "no" to your child he will have learned the same thing.

- It is impossible to find the exact shade of black or blue when you are matching socks or the same combination of colors at the top of white socks.

- Should you forbid your children to watch TV they will pick up books more often, but often to throw at one   another.

A crying child can be heard over a parade band.

- Kids' Senior Class parties go on until their college homecoming.

- When your son drives up in the middle of the night you have mixed emotions. You'd rather it wasn't his car that sounds like that but you're relieved he is home.

- Their fighting won't let up until the rain lets up.

- Your dream of going back to work dies when the rabbit dies.

- When you get the last dish put away someone will want ice cream.

- Your son will discover his term paper is missing right after the garbage has been hauled away.

- Just when your daughter gets a "No Cavities" report she'll chip a tooth.

- If everyone ever agrees on the same TV show it will be pre-empted.

- When your daughter finds a confirmation dress she likes it will not be available in her size.

- When your son takes the car alone for the first time you will hear a siren that will make you a nervous wreck until he gets back.

- When you have fixed a meal with all four food groups your kids will be off with their groups.

- During the two minutes you leave your toddler outside unattended your mother-in-law will drive by.

- Right after you get home from having a professional manicure a child will get a knot in his shoelace.

- The only time there is peace and quiet is when they are plotting something that will disturb peace and quiet.

- A low price will only be on an item of clothing of which your child has a low opinion.

- The missing shoe will not show up until after it no longer fits.

Chapter 22
Surly to Bed, Surly to Rise

They're no longer pleased with Mom and Dad
They yearn for their removal.
But somehow they must face the fact
You don't take parents on approval.

While adolescents are gaining their individuality it is impossible to continuously be at peace with them. They are leaving childhood and entering adulthood and unpleasantness is part of the process. If they don't become ornery they will never become capable of making decisions. When they are 50 they will be going through a cafeteria line, ending up with only silverware and a napkin.

It's the "Ya can't win" age. A teen-ager should wear a T-shirt that says YIELD. They are mentally hissing and booing every statement you make. If you get an answer on Jeopardy they think the show has made a mistake. The only way you can get a civil response from them is to learn ventriloquism.

The following is a typical scene between a mother and teen-age daughter:

DAUGHTER: What are we having for lunch?

MOTHER: Chili. (She is putting it in a bowl for her.)

DAUGHTER: I don't like chili!
(Mother keeps putting chili into bowl.)

DAUGHTER: I don't like chili, I said!
(Mother stops putting chili in bowl.)

DAUGHTER: Is that all I get?!

84

Their smiles are rationed to one every six months.

You who are footing their bills, worrying over every sickness, lamenting every one of their misfortunes get one-word answers and eyes rolled heaven-ward.

The following are some symptoms of adolescence:

- They are neither a morning nor a night person.
- If you say, "Please stir what's on the stove — it's burning" they'll give you a martyr's look.
- They criticize your yawn and your sneeze.
- They do genealogy and leave you out of the family tree.
- The only time they don't slam the door is when they're sneaking in.
- They take, "Just say No" to apply to everything you suggest.
- They hate everyone over 30 because they refuse to judge teen-agers as individuals.
- They think their father gargles louder than other kids' fathers.

- When you are with them it's the opposite of a rap session.
- Their smiles are rationed to one every six months.
- They never say, "Hold that thought" if your conversation with them is interrupted.

You must remember that your teen-ager is not unique. The following are some common statements of parents about their teen-agers:

- "I think her bad posture is from always slinking down in the seat so she won't be seen in the car with me."
- "When she blew out the candles I knew she was wishing for a different mother."
- "She bought green contacts so she wouldn't have my blue eyes."
- "He should chip in on the cost of my hair coloring because he caused my gray hair."
- "She cut her head out of our family picture."
- "Suddenly I feel like I should check blood types to make sure he's our child."
- "She blames everything on birth order and she's an only child.
- "It seems like he sees some checkered flag no one else sees every time he gets in the car."

It would be nice if you could put the teen-age years on fast forward. Since you can't, try to think as little as possible about the unreasonableness and abuse you take. The following are a few more suggestions that might help you get through this ordeal:

- Don't try to joke with him like saying, "Now there's some of your music I like" when there is static.
- Frame your diplomas and hang them in her room.
- Read and re-read the Mother's Day card you got from him.
- Look in the photo album to see her smiling.
- Except on school days let him wake up naturally. Adopt the motto "Let a sleeping teen-ager lie."
- Get your dog to like you. There's a chance your daughter might respect his opinion.

This same offspring who is so ornery with you is apt to be elected President of the Class. Of course you will find out about it by reading it in the paper.

Chapter 23

She Feels Undressed Without a Phone on her Ear

No matter what you think
It's not something you can own
Please remember this —
It is a family phone.

If the prosecutor asked a teen-ager on the witness stand, "Where were you on the night of August 10" and the teen-ager answered, "I was on the telephone from 6:00 until midnight," every person on the jury would believe it.

It is said that Alexander Graham Bell had second thoughts about his invention when his children became teen-agers.

Teen-agers do 90% of their visiting with friends on the telephone. If you suddenly get letters instead of calls from out of town relatives check how long your teen-agers are on the phone.

Both boys and girls spend hours on the phone but this chapter will deal with a **girl** who is a phonoholic.

It might help to know that all mothers suffer telephone problems. Many a mother feels like picketing her daughter on the phone.

The following are some typical comments by mothers regarding the phone situation:

- "We have the busiest busy signal in town."
- "She'll never get arrested because she knows she'd be allowed only one phone call."
- "When she was in my womb I'm sure she kicked when the phone rang."
- "I've got to give her credit for a good excuse. She said, 'Hang up?!! I'm talking to Suicide Hot Line'."
- "She put my husband's boss on hold and didn't get back to him for three-quarters of an hour."
- "She makes me feel like I'm eavesdropping when she calls the Telephone Time Lady."
- "I was standing in front of her tapping my watch and she said, 'Shhh'."
- "It really upsets her when she wastes a sexy 'Hello' on one of my friends."

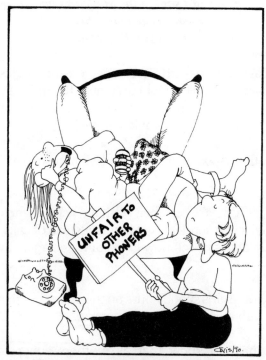

*Many a mother feels like picketing
her daughter on the phone.*

- "When she makes a long-distance call I set an egg timer by her and she always yells, 'Your eggs are done!' and goes right on talking."

There are natural differences between the way an adult and a teen-ager views the phone. If the telephone rings at 3:00 A.M. an adult immediately wonders, "Who died?", a teen-ager, "Who broke up."

The phone situation with a teen in the house will never be good but there could be improvements:

- The call waiting signal should be a loud continuous shriek that couldn't be ignored.

- There could be phones installed in school lockers and on bicycles to cut down on home phone use.

Of course you can't tear gas your daughter off the phone but with a little creative thinking you might possibly achieve this feat in a non-violent way. The following are some suggestions:

- Burn something so the smoke alarm goes off and she can't hear.

- Call the radio station on a neighbor's phone and request her favorite song.

- Point to the D and F on the phone dial to hint she should get at her homework.

- Put an amplifier on the chimes of your clock.

The following are a few rules to follow so you can co-exist more comfortably with your daughter and the phone:

- Don't ever make the error of mistaking a boy caller for a girl.

- Don't ever tell your daughter that a boy called for her if you neglected to get his name.

- When you hand a message to her while she's on the phone print it with magic marker in huge letters or she won't bother to read it.

Try to make a rule that after she says, "Good-bye" she must hang up and not add, "Oh, by the way.." However don't be too hopeful she will follow this. Probably as far as you can go in making telephone rules is "No calls from 3:00 to 4:00 AM."

Chapter 24

They Want to be Taken Seriously and They Look like That?

You got him to wear a suit
You're so happy you could clap
But after just a minute
He dons a baseball cap.

Teen-agers blissfully expect to be accepted with hair and clothes that look terrible. Why they want to look their worst is a mystery. Perhaps it's their way of hitting a spoon against a glass and saying, "Ladies and Gentlemen, may I please have your attention!"

There is a no more difficult task in parenting than getting an adolescent to get his hair cut. It seems that much hair must be against the fire code.

The following are a couple of suggestions of how to get your teen-ager to get his hair cut:

- Speak softly. There's a remote chance he may think the hair is interfering with his hearing.

- Tell him, "If you ever decide to run for office and they put a picture of you looking like that in the paper it will ruin your political career."

*The only way I can tell if he's been in
a fight is if there are blood stains,
because his jeans are always ripped.*

You never worry about having long-lasting material in their clothing because you hope it won't last.

"You think you look sexy in that? It seems to me that outfit would do more to discourage sex than the fear of AIDS" is something you can't say. Other things that come to mind but you'd better not say are:

- "That's an outfit you'd wear to apply for a job you want to make sure you don't get."
- "It's obvious you didn't use Edith Head. In fact it's obvious you didn't use any head."
- "Was this premeditated? Did you lay that out last night?"
- "Are you going to wear that where there are people?"
- "Shouldn't you be advertising something?"
- "Was the bulb burned out in the dressing room where you bought that?"

There isn't much you can do at this time but the following are a few suggestions that might make it a little easier on your aesthetic nature:

- Try to have him go out for a sport. He'll at least look good while he's in uniform.

- Keep saying over and over to yourself, "It's a phase."

- Seat him in a low chair at the table so you see less of what he's wearing.

- Show him a picture of himself when you still had control and he was well dressed with a neat haircut so he'll see how much better he looked. However, cover up your purpose by saying something like, "Look at this picture of our house when it still had its porch."

- Don't ask her why she wants to look like that. Express approval as you would of a friend. Yours is not to question why — yours is but to view and lie.

- Suggest that he put his clothes on layaway at stores. If there is time to think it over he may change his mind.

- Tell her to stand in the back row when they take the class picture no matter how short she is.

- Tell him that outfit accentuates his acne.

Every parent has the same feelings about their children's appearances. The following are a few typical comments:

- "I said to him, 'It's fine to wear that fluorescent shirt when you're out jogging at night, but not to your grandfather's retirement party'."

- "If I look right into his eyes I can avoid looking at his clothes, but it's almost impossible not to see his hair."

92

- "I asked him if he'd wear a T-shirt that says, 'I'VE GOT GOOD CLOTHES IN MY CLOSET'."

- "I can't believe he has girls calling him. Of course they can't see him over the phone but they must see him at school."

- "I said to her, 'We spent $3,000 having those teeth straightened and we're not having them covered up by bangs'."

- "I wouldn't mind so much if he hogged the bathroom in the morning if his appearance showed he hogged the bathroom."

- "I wish they'd print the list of his activities over his picture instead of beside it in the yearbook."

- "He says the First Amendment lets him dress like that."

- "The only way I can tell if he's been in a fight is if there are blood stains because his jeans are always ripped."

It helps not to laugh to think your money paid for those awful clothes.

Chapter 25

You Can't be a
Surrogate Applicant

*Every practical mother
Thinks it very funny
A son works hard to earn a letter
But hates to work hard to earn money.*

Looking for a job when you finish school is not a new idea but one that is often hard to get through to your son or daughter.

This chapter will deal with a **son** who is stuck at the starting gate.

It is very difficult to convert a party animal into a work horse but it is a necessary project.

You will have to work extra hard if your son is lazy as well as being fun loving. The following are a couple of signals that you have a lazy son:

- When he had a Kool-Aid stand he sold packages of Kool-Aid instead of making them up.

- If there were no clean glasses in the cupboard instead of washing one he used a dice cup from a game.

You must tell your son he has to go out and apply for a job — prospective employers do not make house calls.

The following are some suggestions to make your son go out and get a job:

- Write "Apply for a job" on his chore list.

- Ask him, "Do you want to use your brief case only for resumes forever?"

- Tell him there are no car deals offering "Nothing down and no payments until you get a job."
- Tell him he can borrow your car on the days he goes for an interview and keep it the rest of the day.
- Vacuum four or five times a day. He may get tired lifting his feet.
- Tell him even his dog will respect him more if he has a job.
- Get him some business cards with just his name. He will be anxious to get something else on them.

Many excuses will be given for his not going out to look for a job. The following are a few examples of statements you don't want to hear:

- "I couldn't find the Help Wanted ads in last night's paper. I think they forgot to print them."

Your child is lazy if when he had a Kool-Aid stand he sold packages of Kool-Aid instead of making them up.

- "I'm having second thoughts about going for this interview today."

- "I'm going to just goof off during my interview today."

You can't have an artist sketch a picture of how he would look in a suit and with a neat haircut and have him give it to a prospective employer along with his application. You can't sit in front of your son at an interview and flip cards like teleprompters do. You cannot be so desperate you suggest to your son that he tell a prospective employer he is his real father.

But there are things you can do so your son will be successful in his pursuit of a job:

- Hunt until you find a pen. Don't let him fill out the application in pencil or crayon.

- De-fish his handshake.

- Even if he promises not to blow a bubble tell him he shouldn't chew gum.

- Be sure he knows how to spell the name of the street he lives on and his zip code number.

- Tell him to be optimistic but not so much so that he parks in the Employees' parking lot and especially not in the Executive parking lot.

- Tell him he should not put a check in the square after HAVE YOU EVER BEEN CONVICTED OF A FELONY just to look macho.

- Hide his boom box so he doesn't take it to the interview with him.

- Tell him that no matter how long the interview goes he shouldn't say, "I'd love to stay and talk to to you but I have other commitments."

- Invite all his friends over to the house for the next few days so he won't be on the phone when someone calls about a job.

You can just hope he gets a job before he outgrows the clothes you bought him to wear to interviews.

Chapter 26
Don't Write her College Accomplishments in her Baby Book

She'd rather party than study
She's the opposite of a scholar.
It doesn't bother her that tuition
Is making you live in squalor.

Having a son or daughter go off to college is part of the child-raising process. In this chapter a daughter will be used as an example of what to expect.

You should be happy that your daughter has chosen to attend college. Some young women want to go out and make money right after high school and some girls have been known to delay college until their acne cleared up.

You have to accept the unpleasantness that goes with her attaining a higher education. You probably will not have to scrub floors but you probably will have to scrub lavish vacations and expensive cars.

Even if the dog is hers you will be stuck caring for it after she leaves. Chances are extremely remote the college will adopt it as the school mascot.

You can't expect instant improvement when your daughter goes away to school. In fact things might get worse before they get better. Her ripped jeans will have longer rips and the T-shirts off the shoulder will go further down the shoulder. She won't speak in a cultured manner immediately. In fact when she argues she will use new four-letter words.

She asks you to visit campus during Spring break.

Even if you build a wing on the college you will not be permitted to leave her belongings there over the summer. When you pick her up she always has 50% more stuff than when you brought her in the Fall.

Daughters in college have a very low threshold of embarrassment when it comes to mothers. They feel they should get college credit for asking you to visit. Two blocks from college, even with all her luggage, she'll say (or want to say), "Drop me off here."

There can be signals to look for so you know that she is embarrassed by you:

- She asks you to visit campus during Spring break.

- You attend a college function with her and she insists a name tag will ruin your dress.

- She says, "I'll keep your name tag in my purse — if you wear it you might lose it and you won't have it as a souvenir."

- You're walking along and as friends approach she stops to tie her shoelace and she's wearing moccasins.

- She puts her coat over her head while she's walking with you and it's not raining.

When this happens you should try to remember when she was a little kid and she was running after you yelling, "Wait up, Mom!"

Many daughters gain a lot of weight when they go off to college as their diet suddenly consists mainly of fast food which is loaded with calories. A mother is bound to hound when her daughter is round. Unfortunately, however, a mother's words about weight carry no weight. Therefore it is better to give her the message in subtle ways that she should watch her intake of food:

- Leave her floor as cluttered as it is. There is a chance she will have to step on her scale to get to bed.

- Mirror your dining room so she can view herself as she eats.

- Get violent when she comes in late. She may want to lose weight so sneaking in will be easier.

- Tell her it is better to have her body shown via a bikini than ripped jean seams.

- Explain to her that the body who breaks chairs will not break hearts.

The following are some suggestions to help you get through your daughter's college experience:

- Hide your clothes that she often borrows at a friend's house while she is packing.

- Subscribe to **Soap Opera News** so she doesn't cut class to find out what's happening on her Soap.

- Pack Band-Aids. She may cut class because she has a blister.

- Get her a flattering mirror. She might cut class because she doesn't think she looks good.

- Teach her to read while walking so she can study while walking during student protests.

- Get her a helmet with her school colors. If she goes on a motorcycle she is more apt to wear it.

- Put a time limit on how long she can call home every night to see if she had any phone calls.

- Tell her to forget what you said about always being sure to drink plenty of liquids. She might choose the wrong liquids.

- Have pencil and paper with you when you are with her on campus. You may not be able to hear each other over the loud music.

- You are fantasizing if you expect a voice on her answering machine to say, "I can't come to the phone right now because I'm studying."

There are also things you should **not** do in order to have the best success with a daughter in college. For instance you can't have the FBI run a check on her prospective roommate. Other taboos are:

- Don't frame her college acceptance letter. You must wait for the diploma.

- Don't rush her. Don't give her a gold case for business cards when she's only a freshman.

- Don't find out the time of her morning classes and call her early every morning if she has a roommate.

- Don't have a cheery hello when you answer your phone. If your daughter is on the other end she'll think you're having a better time there and want to come home for the weekend.

Does spending thousands of dollars to send your daughter to college mean you don't have to pay back the I.O.U. you put in her piggy bank? No!

Chapter 27

Dictionary of a Mad Mother

In describing your emotions
It's hard to find the words which fit,
But when you do all mothers
Join you and say, "That's it!"

Emotions commonly experienced by mothers are misery and desperation. The following are situations that define these emotions:

- Misery is seeing your child come out with a box of soda crackers as you are putting away the vacuum.
- Misery is getting stuck in a department store elevator when taking your kids to the restroom.
- Misery is getting to the check-out counter and finding that your discount coupons were made into confetti by your child in the cart.
- Misery is having your child ineligible for kindergarten by one day.
- Misery is having the power go off while your daughter is blow drying her hair for a date.
- Misery is typing your child's absence excuse at the last minute and finding your fingers were on the wrong keys.
- Misery is having the boy with whom your son shares apartment expenses at college be his brother.
- Misery is having your children eat so much of the cake batter that you can only bake one cupcake.

- Misery is having to tell your husband that your daughter made the hammock into a poncho.
- Misery is having your three-year old print his name over a double page of the bride's guest book.
- Misery is having your child say, "How come?!" in front of guests when you ask to wash his hands for dinner.
- Misery is telling your child to take a few steps to see if shoes fit and have him take off running through the mall and come back and say they don't.
- Misery is cleaning your son's room and finding four books on hang gliding.
- Misery is being out of Band-Aids when your child comes in bleeding and your mother-in-law is there.
- Misery is having it start to rain just as the TV breaks.
- Misery is finding out that your child makes it impossible to get substitutes for his class.

***Misery is having your child break the ribbon
that was supposed to be cut by the mayor.***

- Misery is having your child break the ribbon that was supposed to be cut by the mayor.

- Misery is having your son laugh at your other son's new jacket.

- Desperation is letting your daughter use your wig for a shower cap.

- Desperation is Scotch-taping together pieces of tissue paper encasing fruit to wrap a present for a birthday party.

- Desperation is using a pipe cleaner for a shoe lace.

- Desperation is giving your daughter a pencil case when she needs an evening bag.

- Desperation is telling your son that the teacher he hates was once a Playboy Bunny.

- Desperation is taking down wet laundry so your daughter can have a jump rope.

- Desperation is packing your son's lunch in a 30-gallon garbage bag.

- Desperation is having your kindergartener take your pre-schooler for Show and Tell.

- Desperation is sending an 1873 Silver Dollar for lunch money.

- Desperation is asking the librarian to meet you at the library in the middle of the night so your son can get the book he needs.

- Desperation is sleeping all night in front of the church rummage sale so you can buy back your daughter's sweater that you donated.

- Desperation is siphoning gas from a neighbor's car so you can drive your kids to school.

Chapter 28

Maxims Give Words Maximum Strength

Socrates and Aristotle thought thoughts
That are well to bear in mind,
But a mother can surpass these gems
Going through her daily grind.

It is said that children carry a lot of baggage from their homes as they go into life. This has a negative connotation. There could also be good baggage. One example of good baggage would be proverbs. Children will heed your advice to hang onto their money much more readily if you say, "A penny saved is a penny earned" than if you simply say, "Save your money."

You will go through motherhood better if facts are made catchy.

The following are some truisms woven into maxims:

- Parents give their children the ammunition with which they shoot off their mouths.

- Read to your children — something besides the riot act.

- Don't let the last pat on the back you give your child be for burping.

- If you always give your child free rein he won't know what you mean if you ever say, "Whoa!"

- Ignoring is bliss.

- Never having to say you're sorry means you don't have children.

If you always give your child free rein,
he won't know what you mean if you ever say "Whoa!"

- School is the place you send your children to improve their minds so you won't lose yours.

- If in the other room they're quiet — don't buy it.

- Kids think their friends are good sources of advice. Parents think their friends are good sources of vice.

- If you can't have an open mind about what your children are doing at least have one that is slightly ajar.

- Children today are creatures of grab it.

- A mother has to live down her kids living it up.

- A mother has a sixth sense that her kids don't have any.

- You wait on kids hand and foot and they cost you an arm and a leg.

- In order to have children who succeed parents shouldn't intercede.

- During the teen years children put their parents on hold.

- A mother who always calls a child the right name only has one child.

- Kids will go that extra mile so they won't be seen with their parents.

- If you ever do have a meeting of the minds with your teen-ager it will be adjourned in record time.

- What used to be considered Mother's intuition is now considered Mother's intrusion.

- To a child a mother is someone who pats other people's children on the head and her own on the seat.

- Kids think money grows on trees and there is always a bumper crop.

- Your daughter is a built-in baby-sitter only until the boys notice she is "built."

- Family life is where seclusion is delusion.

- Children are like ants — they get into everything in the cupboard except the cleaning supplies.

- If you continually harp, your child will wish you were playing one.

- A baseball diamond is a mother's best friend.

- Kids go from one phase right into another. They are never phased out.

Chapter 29

They Take the Flight and You Experience the Turbulence

When they leave emergency numbers
What's the worst one to omit?
No, it's not the family doctor,
It's another person that can sit.

Years ago there weren't credit cards so couples didn't take long vacations and if men went to conventions they didn't take their wives with them so long-term baby-sitting wasn't needed.

Today it is, and grandmothers are often called upon to perform this noble and difficult task. The rate of burn-out is high and you can't let the flame die out until the parents get back.

Just because you can keep your eye on four Bingo cards doesn't mean you can watch four kids so you should consider refusing.

A grandmother rightly feels the parents will be less upset if she offers an excuse instead of just saying, "No." The following are a few suggestions for excuses:

- "My memory is so bad I wouldn't be able to remember where they'd tell me they'd be right after school."

- "I'm in a play at the Senior Citizens' Center and we have to practice all day long every day and every evening."

- "I've got five books from the library and I want to finish reading them. When you're on a fixed income you can't have library fines."

- "If I came I would never know if you like me for myself or because I baby-sit."

- "I do house-sitting but I don't do baby-sitting."

Most times it's better to do it than suffer the guilt you feel after you refuse and with some thought this valiant act can be made easier.

First, even though it's a second honeymoon let the parents know they can't have an un-disclosed destination like they did for their first honeymoon.

Then be sure you know how many baby aspirin it takes to make a regular one in case you forget to pack yours.

Don't be surprised if your grandchild cries until the parents give him the present they brought for you.

109

You are better off if you face the fact your precious grandchildren are regular red-blooded kids. Don't fantasize situations that will not occur. For instance the following are some statements you will never hear:

- "If it's too much trouble, Grandma, don't bother."
- "You already told me that, Grandma, but it bears repeating."
- "You don't have to give me my allowance that is due today. Money would cheapen our relationship."
- "We have a lot of things to discover about each other this week.

You will be using an alternate approach to punctuality. At the time when you would have already been at your destination an hour you will be leaving your house to get there.

Someday a baby-sitting grandmother will be able to punch up her grandchild's name on a computer and the screen will show his pet peeves, foods to which he is allergic, kids he can't get along with, favorite toys, subjects with which he needs help and what will get him to go to bed. But now you must develop your own best methods of survival.

It is important for the sake of the child's self-esteem that you don't let the child know that taking care of him is difficult. The following are a few no-no's:

- Don't tie yellow ribbons around trees.
- Don't keep setting the timer so you'll know another hour has passed.
- Don't put stars and other symbols of happiness on the date the parents are returning.
- Don't hang up the parents' vacation brochure and throw darts at it.

One of the worst things that can happen is having the child cry because he misses his parents. Besides if you see him crying because his parents are gone you are apt to cry too — and louder. The following are some tips that will help avoid this unpleasantness:

- Don't airplane spoons full of food into the child's mouth. It will remind him of his parents taking off.
- Don't let them hear their parents' voices unless the parents are on their way home and less than a block from the home. When the parents call say that the child is busy finger painting and can't hold the phone.

When you've got a good thing going you want to keep it going and having them asleep is certainly in that category. Therefore it is natural to take precautions to prevent the child from being awakened.

However some grandmothers have gone overboard in not disturbing a child in slumber. There have been cases of grandmothers sleeping in a chair in the living room or bunking in the bathtub to avoid walking past his bedroom door. One grandmother asked a neighbor to take down her wind chimes. The following are some additional suggestions to help you on a long-term baby-sitting job:

- Fine them every time they say, "Mommy let's us."
- Fine them every time they say something nice about the other grandma.
- If they ask a question instead of answering it say, "Look it up." This keeps them busy. Don't let vanity cause you to give the answer.
- Fax report cards to the parents.
- Don't worry if they only eat junk food. They can't get serious malnutrition in a week.
- When a child has a tummy ache tell him to think of all the parts of his body that don't ache.
- Have them make a new WELCOME HOME sign every day.
- Watch the weather channel. If your weather is bad you might drive where the weather would permit them to be outside.
- Ordinarily it's against Grandmother Rules to say, "Put it back" when shopping but not when you're doing long-term baby-sitting.
- Tell yourself the trip is saving the marriage.
- Have something wonderful planned for yourself when the sitting is over to make it easier for you to get through the week. (Of course it would have to be something like a trip around the world or a shopping spree in Paris.)
- Cancel your beauty parlor appointment so you look more harrassed when the parents get home.

There are also a few rules regarding the parents' return:

- No matter how happy you are to see them don't hug them excessively hard. They will probably be sunburned.
- Don't give a completely grim report. Try to have one humorous anecdote.
- Don't strangle them with their leis even in fun.

Don't be surprised if your grandchild cries until the parents give him the present they brought for you.

Please send me ⎯⎯⎯⎯⎯ copies of this book at $4.95 ea. plus $1.75 per book for postage. Enclosed is my check money order for $⎯⎯⎯⎯⎯⎯⎯.

Please make checks payable to:

LOU DUFFY PRODUCTIONS

Name ⎯⎯⎯⎯⎯⎯⎯⎯⎯⎯⎯⎯⎯⎯⎯⎯⎯⎯⎯⎯⎯⎯⎯⎯

Address ⎯⎯⎯⎯⎯⎯⎯⎯⎯⎯⎯⎯⎯⎯⎯⎯⎯⎯⎯⎯⎯⎯

City ⎯⎯⎯⎯⎯⎯⎯⎯⎯ State ⎯⎯⎯⎯⎯ Zip Code ⎯⎯⎯

Send this form and your payment to:

Lou Duffy Productions
439 Eisenhower Avenue
Janesville, Wisconsin   53545

⎯ ⎯

Please send me ⎯⎯⎯⎯⎯ copies of this book at $4.95 each plus $1.75 per book for postage. Enclosed is my check or money order for $⎯⎯⎯⎯⎯⎯⎯.

Please make checks payable to:

LOU DUFFY PRODUCTIONS

Name ⎯⎯⎯⎯⎯⎯⎯⎯⎯⎯⎯⎯⎯⎯⎯⎯⎯⎯⎯⎯⎯⎯⎯⎯

Address ⎯⎯⎯⎯⎯⎯⎯⎯⎯⎯⎯⎯⎯⎯⎯⎯⎯⎯⎯⎯⎯⎯

City ⎯⎯⎯⎯⎯⎯⎯⎯⎯ State ⎯⎯⎯⎯⎯ Zip Code ⎯⎯⎯

Send this form and your payment to:

Lou Duffy Productions
439 Eisenhower Avenue
Janesville, Wisconsin   53545